THE GARDENS AUDLEY END

MICHAEL SUTHERILL, MSC
Historic Properties, English Heritage

Gardens, like houses, make statements about their owners and the times in which they lived. This is certainly the case at Audley End: from the Middle Ages onwards the house has been adapted and remodelled to reflect the changing tastes of its owners. The history of the landscape has been no less eventful, with new generations vigorously rejecting the innovations of their predecessors. The way in which the landscape has developed is not only a question of fashion, but reflects underlying philosophical concerns about man and his relationship with nature.

Coade Stone tripod based on a model from classical antiquity

In the Middles Ages the Benedictine Abbey of Walden was built where the house now stands. The abbey had an extensive estate, which was cultivated for raw materials. In this period nature was regarded as a resource, and cultivation for purely aesthetic reasons was limited.

After the dissolution of the monasteries the abbey buildings were converted into a private house. By the early 1600s this had been replaced by a vast mansion (of which the present house is only a part). The owner was Thomas Howard, first Earl of Suffolk. To provide a suitable setting for his new house Suffolk created a great formal garden consisting of straight alleys and rectangular ponds, with long avenues of trees stretching out into the countryside. These formal gardens represent the height of artificiality in the history of Audley End's landscape, and expressed man's desire to impose order on his environment.

Audley End's most notable eighteenth-century owner, Sir John Griffin Griffin (later fourth Lord Howard de Walden and first Baron Braybrooke), had very different ideas. The landscape park which he created is a fine example of the 'natural' or 'informal' style in gardening, and was largely devised by its most famous exponent, 'Capability' Brown. The mid-eighteenth century in England was a time of peace, optimism and growth. Developments in natural philosophy inspired the belief that the world operated in a rational, harmonious way and that man and nature could co-exist peacefully. These ideas were expressed in the writings of the great philosophers and garden theorists of the day, who rejected the suppression of nature and called for a natural, unfettered style. Under Brown's supervision the park at Audley End was transformed, as barriers were broken down to allow views across the acres of gently rolling pasture which lay beyond the old formal gardens.

This magnificent eighteenth-century park remains substantially as it was when first created. An exception is the formal flower garden or parterre that was added in the 1830s by the third Lord Braybrooke. By this time the ideals that had inspired the natural style had faded. Political turbulence at the end of the eighteenth century had dashed confidence and created a renewed desire for order. Ironically the story might seem to have come full circle, back to the formality of the Jacobean era. Yet the parterre is itself a romantic interpretation of its Jacobean predecessors. This fanciful, selective drawing on the past was as much a symbol of the age as the changes Sir John had undertaken in the previous century.

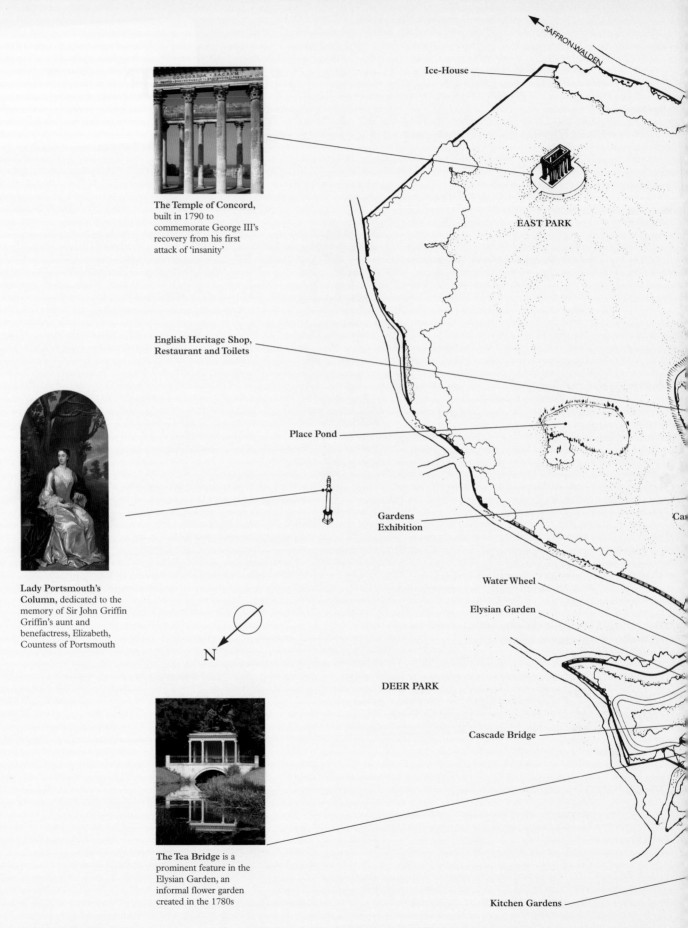

The Temple of Concord, built in 1790 to commemorate George III's recovery from his first attack of 'insanity'

Lady Portsmouth's Column, dedicated to the memory of Sir John Griffin Griffin's aunt and benefactress, Elizabeth, Countess of Portsmouth

The Tea Bridge is a prominent feature in the Elysian Garden, an informal flower garden created in the 1780s

Ice-House

SAFFRON WALDEN

EAST PARK

English Heritage Shop, Restaurant and Toilets

Place Pond

Gardens Exhibition

Water Wheel

Elysian Garden

DEER PARK

Cascade Bridge

N

Kitchen Gardens

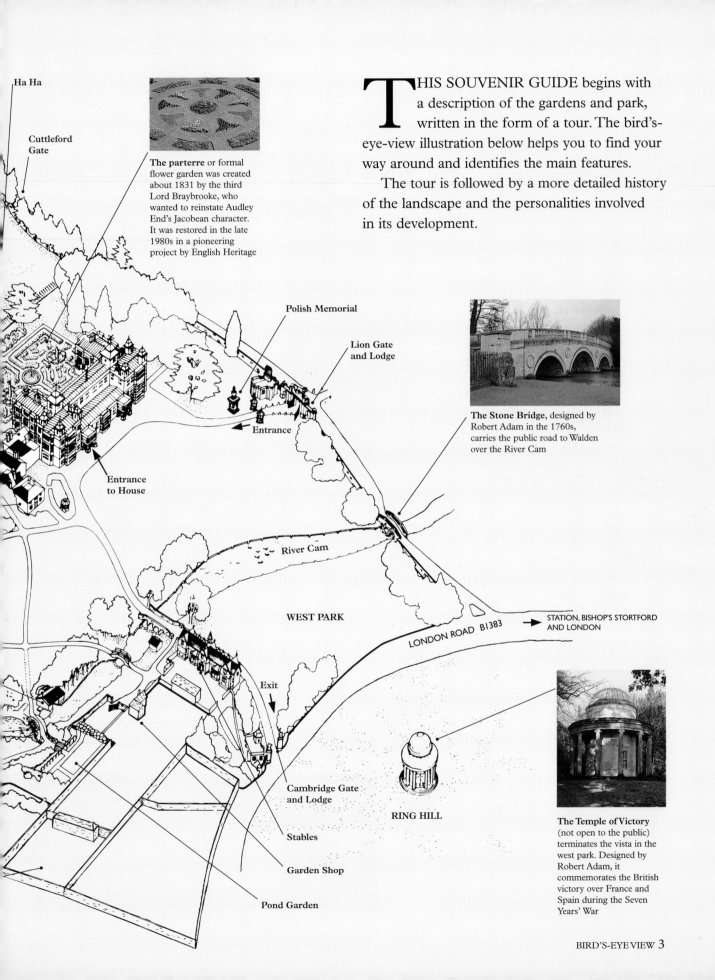

THIS SOUVENIR GUIDE begins with a description of the gardens and park, written in the form of a tour. The bird's-eye-view illustration below helps you to find your way around and identifies the main features.

The tour is followed by a more detailed history of the landscape and the personalities involved in its development.

Ha Ha

Cuttleford Gate

The parterre or formal flower garden was created about 1831 by the third Lord Braybrooke, who wanted to reinstate Audley End's Jacobean character. It was restored in the late 1980s in a pioneering project by English Heritage

Polish Memorial

Lion Gate and Lodge

Entrance

Entrance to House

The Stone Bridge, designed by Robert Adam in the 1760s, carries the public road to Walden over the River Cam

River Cam

WEST PARK

STATION, BISHOP'S STORTFORD AND LONDON

LONDON ROAD B1383

Exit

Cambridge Gate and Lodge

Stables

Garden Shop

Pond Garden

RING HILL

The Temple of Victory (not open to the public) terminates the vista in the west park. Designed by Robert Adam, it commemorates the British victory over France and Spain during the Seven Years' War

ABOVE *Despite modern ploughing, the scale of the park can be appreciated in this view from the Ring Hill. The River Cam is a prominent feature of the west park, while the Temple of Concord dominates the view to the east*

RIGHT *Trees of differing growth rates were chosen, with the faster- and taller-growing species planted in hollows so that when they matured they produced a flat, unbroken horizon line*

THE WEST PARK

The tour of Audley End gardens begins at the entrance front of the house, which overlooks the west park. The view today differs little from that which Sir John Griffin Griffin would have observed shortly before his death in 1797.

However, it is distinctly different from the view he would have seen three decades earlier, when he inherited his aunt's estate at Audley End in 1762. Then, he would have been confronted by rigidly aligned avenues and canals, all enclosed by high walls – the remains of the formal gardens established by the first Earl of Suffolk in the early seventeenth century.

Under Sir John Griffin Griffin the earl's gardens were gradually replaced by a new park in the 'natural' landscape style. The designer and supervisor of these works was Lancelot 'Capability' Brown, the most eminent landscape gardener of his day (see p.25).

Under Brown's supervision the land was graded (remodelled to remove uneven ground) and seeded with grass to produce a smooth sweep of pasture from the house to the western ridge of the Cam valley. Later, numerous trees were planted, including larch, Scotch firs, Weymouth limes, Portuguese laurels, 'Black' Canada larch, Carolina poplar, and Dutch alders. Along the western ridge of the valley a 'belt' of trees was planted across the horizon, creating a sense of seclusion – a private arcadia. Inside the park the techniques of contemporary landscape artists were used: for example, evergreens of a smoke-blue hue were planted at the edges of the woodland belts, their colour giving an illusion of depth.

The effect of a secluded woodland valley was in fact an illusion. Since the Middle Ages the area in front of the house had been intersected by the two public roads which are still present today. The road directly ahead of you once provided the main link between London and Norwich, while the one to your left serves the market town of Saffron Walden. These roads were to prove troublesome to Brown, as was the need for fences to keep livestock inside the park and unwanted visitors out. Both interrupted the seamless vista that was so fundamental to the creation of a natural landscape park. To overcome this difficulty Brown introduced a Ha Ha or ditch on either side of the roads, so concealing them while keeping cattle and the general public in their rightful places.

THE TEMPLE OF VICTORY

In the distance straight ahead of you stands the Temple of Victory, built between 1771 and 1775 to the design of Robert Adam. The temple terminates one of a number of vistas designed to create a pleasurable effect from various viewpoints inside the park.

As well as appearing to advantage from afar, the temple provided an enjoyable stopping point as visitors toured the park. Here they could take tea, listen to music, or simply spend time deciphering the theme of the plaster ceiling with its emblems from classical mythology. Further entertainment was provided by the nearby menagerie, completed in 1774, which contained a collection of exotic birds (see p.31).

Unfortunately, neither the Temple of Victory nor the menagerie is now accessible to visitors.

THE CARRIAGE DRIVES AND LION GATE

Brown was also responsible for the creation of the sweeping carriage drives which extend from the house to the two main entrance gateways to your left and right. These new carriage drives replaced the straight Jacobean approach road to the house.

The central carriage arch of the Lion Gate dates from the Jacobean period and was once decorated with cresting to match the cresting formerly on the parapets of the house. The brickwork of the carriage arch was finished in a decorative colour scheme of red and white horizontal bands.

The Lion Gate was remodelled about 1768. The two pedestrian entrance gateways on either side of the central arch were added, together with a small porter's lodge (now demolished). The lodge accommodated a

ABOVE *The Temple of Victory*

TOP *This mid-eighteenth-century painting gives a lively sense of activity in the west park. The cattle are prevented from straying on to the public road in the foreground by a Ha Ha (the brick wall visible beyond the road)*

RIGHT *The Lion Gate.*
The parapet above the
central arch is inscribed
'IOAN BARON HOWARD
DE WALDEN RESTORED
AND ORNAMENTED
1786'

OPPOSITE *This painting*
of about 1710 shows the
west park much as it
would have appeared in
the seventeenth century.
Note the straight carriage
drive and decorated gate,
both of which were
replaced in the mid-
eighteenth century

BELOW *1930s'*
watercolour of the Lion
Gate, showing the lodge
built by the third Lord
Braybrooke in 1846

gate keeper, whose job it was to open the gate whenever the blast of a postilion's horn sounded from an approaching carriage.

Lion Gate was again remodelled in 1786 when preparations were being made for a royal visit (which in the event did not take place). Four urns and a single lion were placed above the parapet; they are made of an artificial substance known as Coade Stone, a fired clay-like material which was developed by a Mrs Coade in the mid-eighteenth century as a cheaper but durable alternative to carved stone.

LION LODGE

The mid-eighteenth-century porter's lodge was replaced by the present lodge in 1846. It was built for the third Lord Braybrooke and was designed by the noted Victorian architect Thomas Rickman. (Rickman is best known for having established categories for the major periods of development in English medieval church architecture: Early English, Decorated and Perpendicular.)

THE RIVER CAM

The river is one of the most striking and dominant features of the park. Over the centuries it has undergone dramatic changes to suit the tastes of Audley End's owners.

In the Jacobean period, when the Earl of Suffolk's formal gardens were created, the river was diverted through a newly cut straight channel to create a vast 'canal'.

Beyond the bridge by the stables the river was dammed by the introduction of a mill, and earth embankments (which remain today) were made to contain the raised water levels.

ABOVE *The skiff or felucca was a colourful addition to the river*

TOP *Audley End from the west, by Edmund Garvey, 1782. Note the sweeping curve of the river, and Lady Portsmouth's Column to the left*

The river was again remodelled in the 1760s, when Brown created the more natural sweeping curve which you see today. In Sir John Griffin Griffin's time a brightly painted skiff plied the river, adding variety to the scene.

THE STONE BRIDGE

Completed in 1764 to the design of Robert Adam, the bridge is constructed of brickwork faced with stone. The design was inspired by a reconstruction drawing of an ancient bridge over the river Bacchiglione, Vicenza, produced by the Italian Renaissance architect Andrea Palladio in his influential book *I Quattro Libri dell' Architettura (The Four Books of Architecture)*. However, the parapet of the bridge was remodelled about 1780 by the Milanese architect Placido Columbani, who was then involved in work inside the house.

In the summer of 1940 two concrete chambers were inserted below the carriageway at either end of the bridge. In the event of an invasion they were to be packed with an explosive charge which could be detonated by remote control using the wiring system attached to the chamber. Somewhat implausibly, this feature was one of a number of counter-invasion measures forming part of a defensive chain known as the General Head Quarters Line installed along the eastern and southern flanks of England.

A further feature relating to the GHQ line is the cast-concrete pill box, built to defend the western bank of the Cam.

ABOVE *Robert Adam
(1728–92) designed a
number of buildings in
the park at Audley End*

LEFT *Adam's 1763
design drawing for the
Stone Bridge*

RIGHT *1930s'*
watercolour of the
Cambridge Lodge

ABOVE *The bull's head*
is a device taken from
the Neville family
coat of arms

THE CAMBRIDGE GATE AND LODGE

The Cambridge Gate is the second of the two main entrances to the park. The lodge was built in 1842 for the third Lord Braybrooke to replace an earlier classically styled lodge built for Sir John Griffin Griffin in the 1760s. Lord Braybrooke, like many of his contemporaries, rejected the classical style that had been so popular in Sir John's time, describing it as the 'art [of architecture] at its lowest ebb'. The lodge is of more generous proportions than its eighteenth-century predecessor, and reflects a greater concern for the welfare of estate employees.

The gate itself, built two years later, consists of two octagonal gate posts topped with bulls' heads.

THE STABLE YARD

The stable building is of early sixteenth-century origin, and may incorporate an earlier monastic building. It was certainly fulfilling the role of a stable by the seventeenth century, by which time the two projecting bay windows and the curious brick doorcase at the central entrance had been added.

The stables were extensively remodelled in the late eighteenth or early nineteenth century when new doors were introduced along the front of the building. During the remodelling the present stalls and loose boxes were installed providing stabling for about twenty horses, including racehorses in the nineteenth century.

The stables are divided into four sections which provided separate accommodation for carriage horses, riding horses and 'nags'. Two of the sections contain loose boxes and stalls, the larger loose boxes being reserved almost exclusively for the racehorses. The large room at the centre of the building housed the carriages. The first floor initially provided accommodation for the stable boys but was later used for storing the horses' feed. Opposite the stables stands a further carriage building, dating from about 1830.

Near the entrance to the stable yard is the Head Gardener's house, remodelled in the mid-nineteenth century. In front of the house stand two small greenhouses, the larger of which was built about 1877 by Mackenzie and Moncur, the manufacturers of the palm house at Kew Gardens. Following the road to your left, you come to the garden shop, housed in the former pony stables and cart sheds of the kitchen gardens.

The path to the right of the shop leads to a curbed walk. A set of mid-Victorian sluice-gates on the right was built about 1850 to regulate the river levels. Originally the gates were operated by hand but the system was motorised in the 1970s. The curbed walk is now planted with varieties prescribed in the writings of the mid-nineteenth-century plantsman William Sawrey Gilpin.

THE POND GARDEN

The Pond Garden is in the 'picturesque' style, popular in the mid-nineteenth century, which sought to emulate the rugged alpine scenery of the Lake District, France and Switzerland. The rockery and the two ponds were constructed by James Pulham & Son of nearby Hoddesden. The firm had developed a cement-like material called 'Pulhamite', produced from crushed clay stone, which could be mixed to simulate specific rock types. A sloppy mix of Pulhamite was laid over brickwork and moulded into rock forms, complete with hollows to take ferns and other plants. The rockwork was planted with

the true Shamrock (Oxalis acetosella), Cotyledon umbilicus, Berberis Darwini, and smaller growing ferns – a scheme that is maintained today.

The pond nearest the rockery was once home to a family of otters. The first otter, a female named Paddy, was purchased by Lord Braybrooke in 1867 during a fishing trip to Connemara. On her death she was mounted and is now on display in the natural history collection in the house (case 56). The otter entered its lodge through an entrance arch in the north wall of the pond (to your left as you face away from the rockery). A hatch in the footpath to the left gave the keeper access to the lodge. The fountain in the otter pond is intended to imitate a natural mineral spring. The artificial 'rocky' mound was planted with ferns and mosses.

The second pond is known as the fish pond. In the nineteenth century it was planted with aquatic plants including Richardia aethiopica and Aponogeton distachyon.

In the 1880s the walls and pergola of the garden were clad with climbing shrubs and roses, a tradition that continues today.

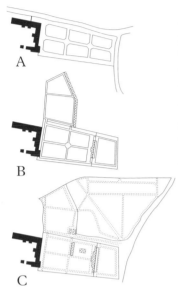

THE KITCHEN GARDENS

A doorway at the end of the Pond Garden gives a view into one of the four enclosures of the kitchen gardens. Throughout their history the kitchen gardens would have been visited by both family and guests as part of their tour of the estate. The pathways were formal and ridged with neatly trimmed edges; each bed would have had a boot scrape to prevent the gardeners from muddying the walks.

The gardens were first established in the 1750s by Elizabeth, Countess of Portsmouth, and extended about 1768 by Sir John Griffin Griffin, who added a second enclosure beyond the one you can see. Sir John built a number of new glass houses and a classical orangery, situated where the nineteenth-century vine house now stands (to your right).

During the early nineteenth century the kitchen gardens were again extended and remodelled. Sir John Griffin Griffin's greenhouses and orangery were demolished in 1802 and the vine house was built. The five bays of the vine house were maintained at different temperatures so that the grapes matured at differing rates.

The kitchen gardens continued to provide produce for the house until the beginning of the Second World War. Since then they have been let to commercial growers.

THE ELYSIAN GARDEN

Returning over the Pond Garden bridge, the path to your left takes you into the Elysian Garden, the remnant of an informal flower garden established for Sir John Griffin Griffin in the early 1780s (see p.32). Designed by Placido Columbani (though based on an earlier scheme by the Essex garden designer and architect Richard Woods), the new garden featured elaborate gateways, temples and statues placed along the route of a circuitous walk. Irregularly shaped flower beds were planted with sweet-smelling flowers, magnolias and azaleas. Orange trees taken from the greenhouse stood in tubs along the walk.

However, the garden proved a frost trap. The flower beds were grassed over about 1830 and a number of the structures demolished. Despite this, the shape of the garden remains intact and several of the eighteenth-century buildings and other features can still be seen.

One such feature is the cascade on your right, designed in 1780 by Richard Woods. As elsewhere on his estate Sir John was actively involved in supervising the work here, often approving the smallest detail. When the masons put up the stones surrounding the cascade, Sir John was called in 'to have the likenof them'; evidently they did not meet with his approval, since they were then taken down and erected in the manner that he prescribed. Columbani's design drawing notes that the great stones of the cascade were to be planted with 'all kinds of Herbaceous Rock plants ... fancifully disposed'.

A further survival from the 1780s is the Tea Bridge, designed by Robert Adam about

1780. The bridge is built of brickwork clad with ashlar stone. The decorative detail was originally made of Liardts cement, a material in which Adam had a financial interest and which he promoted throughout the country. The material proved to be a universal failure, resulting in Adam being sued by a number of his clients. The decorative detail on the Tea Bridge was later replaced with a more durable material.

THE WATER ENGINE

Two small outbuildings house the water-pumping engines. The earlier of the two, in the building nearest the river, was probably installed about 1850 when new technology was being introduced to improve sanitary arrangements in the house. Water was pumped from a nearby natural spring into slate tanks

ABOVE *The Tea Bridge. A card table was kept in the house specifically for use at the bridge*

ABOVE *The water wheel*

LEFT *Design drawing for the cascade, attributed to Richard Woods* on the roof of the house. These gave a good head of water for the various appliances inside. The pump also provided water for the fountains in the gardens.

The engine is driven through a three-gear chain to increase the speed of the pump. The pump is of a three-cylinder design with leather cup pistons (similar to the bicycle pump principle) with leather valves above and below the cylinders.

An alternative engine (in the second outbuilding) was installed about 1900. This employed 'gas engine' technology to power a pump. Paraffin was vaporised and ignited with a hot bulb mounted on the end of the cylinder. Every morning the hot bulb would be heated to red hot by a large industrial blow lamp.

ABOVE *Garden party on the grassed-over parterre, July 1955*

THE PARTERRE GARDEN

The parterre was established on the site of the medieval abbey of Walden, the massive foundations of which still lie beneath the surface. The north range of the Jacobean mansion (to your right as you face it) stands on the foundations of the great abbey church, which extended as far as the Ha Ha behind you.

This area has reflected each of the major developments of the gardens at Audley End. In the seventeenth century, at the time of the Earl of Suffolk's formal gardens, the north and south wings of the house were linked by an arcade or gallery which overlooked a bowling green (where the parterre was later established). In the 1760s, when Lancelot Brown's schemes were put into effect, the area was remodelled to provide an informal flower garden for Lady Griffin (see p.29).

In about 1831, under the third Lord Braybrooke, work began on the creation of a new formal parterre (see p.34). The planting list included geraniums, fuchsia, eschscholtzia and old rose varieties, with evergreen trees providing a backdrop around the outer edges of the garden. The emphasis on herbaceous plants is unusual; later in the century carpet bedding became very popular and eventually replaced much of the original planting in the parterre, which by 1884 required 50,000 plants every year. (A full plant list for the parterre is given on the inside back cover.) The cast-iron fountain at the centre was

ABOVE *The geometric flower beds were inspired by an eighteenth-century pattern book*

RIGHT *The parterre was restored in 1989–90, following extensive research*

brought to Audley End by rail about 1850.

To the far left of the parterre (facing away from the house) stands a Coade Stone tripod, and beside the steps in front of you are two Coade Stone lions. These pieces were moved to their present position from the Elysian Garden about 1830. The tripod is a typically eighteenth-century reference to the classical world: in antiquity tripods were used to support bowls containing offerings to the gods. Here the bowl is supported by three lions' legs surmounted by lions' faces; the overall design of the bowl is based on a stool from the House of Cervi, uncovered during excavations at Herculaneum.

THE MOUNT GARDEN

To the right as you face the park are the remnants of the Mount Garden, laid out in the early 1600s as part of the Earl of Suffolk's formal garden (see p.20). Only the elevated walk and part of the brickwork bastions to the west survive, as this area was also remodelled in the 1760s to form part of Lady Griffin's Garden.

THE EAST PARK

Like the west park, this area appears much as it did in Sir John Griffin Griffin's time, although the 500 deer which roamed freely in the 1790s have long since departed, and part of the park is now occupied by a golf course. To the south the park is bordered by a mown

path; in the eighteenth century there were so many of these paths that twelve gardeners were fully occupied with mowing them, and could scarcely clear them in a week.

In the Jacobean era the east park contained great avenues of trees radiating out into the countryside, but most of these had gone by the time Sir John inherited the estate. Under Sir John, the gently rolling contours of the park were seeded with grass. It was then subdivided (as was common practice) into reserves for cattle, deer and partridges. The fences marking out these reserves were thought intrusive by Prince Puckler Muskau, a notable tourist, who visited Audley End about 1832. The Prince also noted that the deer were quite tame and that the quality of their meat was not as good as those which roamed in the wild.

In the late eighteenth century the park was grazed by Jacobs sheep and polled (hornless) Yorkshire cattle. The cattle were sold in 1811 to be replaced by twenty-three Alderney cows and heifers and one bull.

ABOVE *The house and east park, by William Tomkins, 1788–89. The flower beds of Lady Griffin's Garden can be seen to the left*

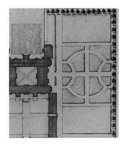

ABOVE *Detail of the Mount Garden, from a drawing by Henry Winstanley of about 1676*

LEFT *Gardeners scything the lawn at Hartwell House, Buckinghamshire*

CONCORDIÆ ⬥ SACRVM

IOAN ⬥ GRIFFIN ⬥ DOM ⬥ HOWARD ⬥ ET ⬥ BRAYBROOKE ⬥ POSVIT ⬥ M ⬥ CC ⬥ C

CUTTLEFORD GATE

This gate probably gave access to the abbey grange or farm which stood in the east park in the medieval period. The pair of octagonal brick gate posts dates from the sixteenth century.

THE ICE-HOUSE

Ice was collected in winter and hauled up from the lake by wagon to the ice-house. It was packed into the deep well with alternate layers of straw, and remained frozen throughout the year.

The ice-house was built in 1836 and probably replaced a mid-eighteenth-century predecessor.

The remainder of the park, beyond the boundary fence, was turned to arable production during the Second World War and continues to be farmed today.

THE TEMPLE OF CONCORD

The temple dominates the view in the east park. It was designed by Robert Furze Brettingham in 1790 to commemorate George III's recovery the previous year from his first attack of porphyria (thought to be insanity at the time).

The twenty Corinthian capitals (the tops of the columns) were supplied by Mrs Coade, as were the two panels set in the entablature (the section above the columns). The panels were described by Mrs Coade as being 'emblematical of the Commercial Advantages etc. resulting from the graces and virtues which surround the Throne'. She also noted that in the centre of the panels is 'a good likeness of His present Majesty'. The king is depicted in the costume of a Roman emperor and the

'commercial advantages' (such as bales of cotton) are supported by figures from Roman mythology. The inscription on the entablature reads:

CONCORDIAE SACRVM IOAN GRIFFIN DOM HOWARD ET BRAYBROOKE POSVIT MDCCXC

[John Griffin Lord Howard and Braybrooke built the Temple of Concord in 1790].

LADY PORTSMOUTH'S COLUMN

Across the park stands the Obelisk, or Lady Portsmouth's Column, which provides a further focal point in the landscape. The design was provided by Robert Adam, and work began in 1773 when a temporary column of timber and plaster was erected, presumably to ensure that the structure could be seen from particular viewpoints in the park.

Once work began on the construction of a stone column in 1774, it proceeded at a tremendous pace: the men were paid for working extra hours and were supplied with beer. The foundations of the column are some 6.1m (20ft) square and 1.5m (5ft) deep. The plinth carries a marble inscription tablet dedicated to the memory of Lady Portsmouth. The column is surmounted by a Portland stone vase which was originally gilded.

PLACE POND

The pond is an artificial lake remodelled in Sir John's time from the largest of the monastic fish ponds. In the Jacobean period it had been a vast canal, with paths along the banks and lines of trees to shade people strolling by the water's edge.

THE DEVELOPMENT OF THE LANDSCAPE

THE MEDIEVAL ABBEY OF WALDEN

RIGHT Eighteenth-century painting of Thomas, Lord Audley of Walden, based on a contemporary portrait

The area in which the park now lies has been occupied since prehistoric times. The Ring Hill, where the Temple of Victory stands, is the site of an Iron Age settlement. In the Roman period a further settlement was established on the banks of the River Cam close to where the house now stands.

In the early twelfth century a Benedictine priory was established on a site which probably lay to the south of the present house. In 1166 the monks abandoned this initial settlement and began building a substantial new stone church and cloister on the site where the house now stands. (Shortly afterwards the priory was raised to the status of an abbey.) Beyond the new buildings, the land was cultivated for use rather than ornament. The high boundary walls enclosed fish ponds, granaries, a mill and a farm, all providing produce for the refectory tables.

THOMAS AUDLEY'S 'CHIEFE AND CAPITOL MANSION HOUSE' (*c*1538–44)

When, in 1533, Henry VIII was excommunicated from the Roman Catholic church he immediately embarked on a programme of dissolving the abbeys and priories. The buildings and lands of Walden Abbey were seized by the Crown and granted to Sir Thomas Audley on 27 March 1538. Audley had served as Speaker of the House of Commons during the Reformation Parliament of 1529–33 and the former abbey was his reward. Like many of his contemporaries he set about creating a residence within the former monastic ranges, and later referred to the remodelled buildings as 'my chiefe and Capitol mansion house'.

ABOVE The Tudor manor house incorporated the buildings of the abbey cloister. The left-hand range was once the nave of the church

A contemporary survey of the estate tells us something about the landscape surrounding this first house at Audley End. The precinct walls of the old abbey were retained, as were a number of the monastic fish ponds which lay to the north of the house. To the east stood a large range of buildings, probably the former monastic grange (farm). To the south a gate lodge gave access on to the road that leads to Saffron Walden, while the river meandered in front of the west precinct wall. Unfortunately the lack of detail in the survey means that we have little idea of the gardens which undoubtedly surrounded this early house.

THE JACOBEAN GARDEN
(*c*1605–26)

Thomas Audley died in 1544 and in due course the house and estate passed to his grandson, Thomas Howard. Howard was a successful soldier, courtier and politician who was knighted by Elizabeth I for gallantry in command of one of the ships which defeated the Armada in 1588. He became Baron Howard de Walden in 1597, and a Knight of the Garter the following year. After the accession of James I in 1603, Howard's fortunes improved still further. Within two months he was created Earl of Suffolk and Lord Chamberlain of the Household, and in 1614 he was elevated to the office of Lord Treasurer.

By the early 1600s Suffolk had become enormously ambitious and foresaw for himself a long career as James's first minister. Since his grandfather's house was insufficiently grand for his new rank, and in the expectation that the king would be a frequent guest, in 1605 he commissioned the construction of one of the largest private residences ever built in Britain.

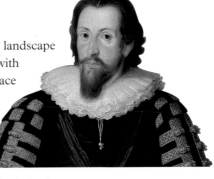

and strict order imposed on the landscape expressed the order of society, with everything having its rightful place in a fixed hierarchy. Avenues and paths all led towards the focal point of the house, whose owner exercised absolute authority over his estate, just as the king exercised absolute power in the country. In the natural hierarchy, too, man came at the top: the rigidity of garden layouts expressed the ideal of man's mastery over nature.

Work on the new gardens probably began about 1614 and continued for at least the next four years. The haphazard arrangement of medieval buildings and field patterns was completely remodelled to create a fashionable, rigidly aligned garden and park.

The area immediately around the new house was divided into a series of self-contained formal gardens in walled enclosures. The largest of the monastic ponds was retained as a vast formal canal some 200m (656ft) long by 50m (164ft) wide. Alongside it lay a 'wilderness' (in fact an ordered plantation, not wild at all) and a cellar (kitchen) garden, while to the east a bowling green was laid out.

ABOVE *Thomas Howard, first Lord Howard de Walden and Earl of Suffolk (1561–1626). His successful career came to an abrupt end in 1618*

Such a vast house required a suitable setting, and Suffolk no doubt wished his new gardens to reflect the latest taste. Seventeenth-century gardens were large, formal and divided up into a number of self-contained walled enclosures, almost like outside rooms. Vast stretches of water were contained in still, rectangular pools. Paths were straight and crossed at right-angles, while avenues of trees radiated out into the distance. The formality

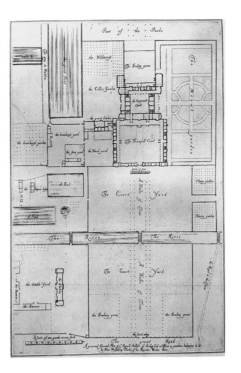

FAR LEFT *Henry Winstanley's drawing of Audley End in 1676 shows the vast scale of the Jacobean mansion*

LEFT *This plan of the seventeenth-century gardens emphasises the rigid layout of all its elements*

South of the house a 'Mount Garden' was created. The Mount was a common feature in Tudor and Jacobean gardens, consisting of a raised bank with a broad walkway on top. Walking was prescribed for exercise in the sixteenth and seventeenth centuries and the Mount at Audley End provided an ideal place for strolling. In bad weather walkers could retire to the shelter of an arcade (covered passageway) in the south range of the house. To the west the elevated walkway of the Mount was retained by a brick wall from which four semicircular bastions projected, adding to the castle-like air of the house.

The monastic fish ponds, now lined with trees, were mainly ornamental although they continued to provide fish for the table.

In the east park the abbey grange (farm) was demolished and great formal avenues of deciduous trees were planted, through which fallow deer roamed. These effectively extended the formality of the garden into the landscape beyond – a further expression of man's control over nature.

Unfortunately the Earl of Suffolk had little opportunity to enjoy his new gardens, for in 1618 he and his wife were convicted of embezzlement and committed to the Tower of London. They were released some nine days later, having agreed to pay a fine of £30,000, but their subsequent financial troubles were so great they could not continue to support the estate they had created, with the result that the gardens and park fell into decline.

The diarist John Evelyn wrote in 1654 that they 'were not in order'.

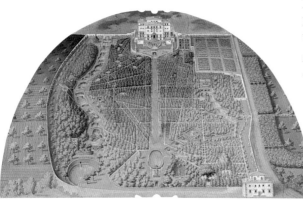

MUSEO DI FIRENZE COM'ERA//SCALA

The river, formerly a meandering trickle, was dammed, transforming it into a broad formal canal. New boundary walls were constructed and two elaborately detailed brick gateways were built, each decorated in bold bands of red and white.

The main approach to the house was via the westernmost of these gateways. A double avenue of lime trees flanked the approach road, which extended from the gateway to the outer court, crossing the river by way of an elaborate bridge. On either side of the river were lawns and two further bowling greens.

A service court was built beside the Great Kitchen, containing a wood yard and brew house, with a hop garden attached. The house was well supplied by its estate: a dovehouse provided fresh meat and eggs; rabbit meat and furs came from a warren on the Ring Hill; and irises were harvested for medicinal purposes from the Flag Pond (so called because the plants were referred to as 'flags').

ABOVE *The Villa di Pratolino near Florence. The design of Suffolk's formal gardens was influenced by the great contemporary gardens of Europe*

The gardens were enclosed by rigidly aligned **boundary walls**

Elaborate brick gateways were decorated in bands of red and white

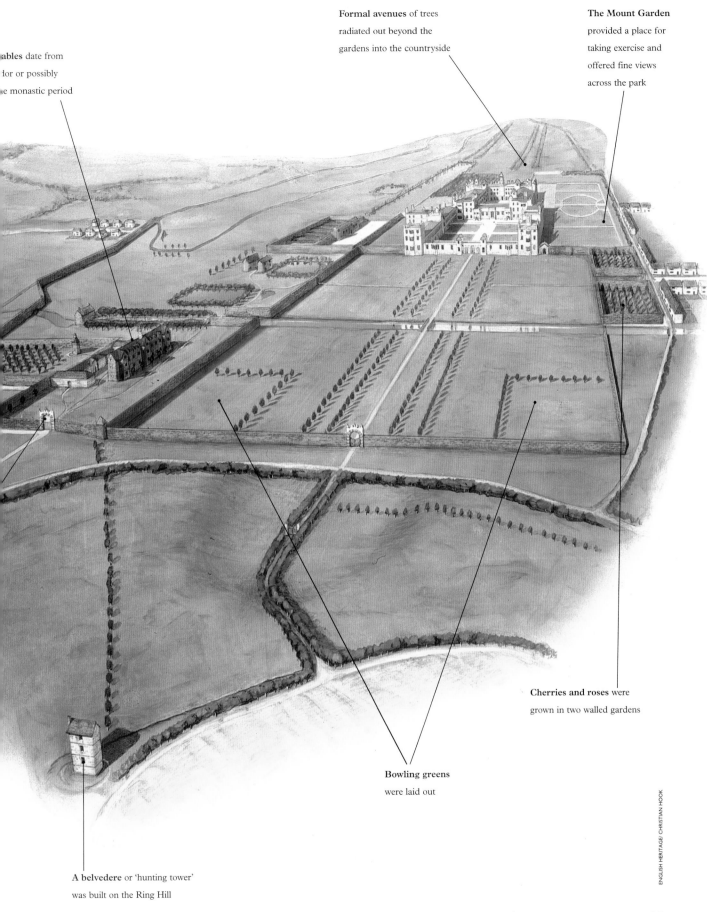

Formal avenues of trees radiated out beyond the gardens into the countryside

The Mount Garden provided a place for taking exercise and offered fine views across the park

...**ables** date from
...for or possibly
...e monastic period

Cherries and roses were grown in two walled gardens

Bowling greens were laid out

A belvedere or 'hunting tower' was built on the Ring Hill

ENGLISH HERITAGE/ CHRISTIAN HOOK

RIGHT *The king was probably attracted to Audley End by its proximity to the racecourse at Newmarket*

ABOVE *Charles II made few changes to the layout of the Earl of Suffolk's gardens*

RIGHT *Sir John Vanbrugh (1664–1726)*

A ROYAL PALACE (1668–1701)

Suffolk died in May 1626, leaving his successors to bear the twin burdens of his debts and the enormous costs of maintaining his vast property. In 1668 the house and the immediate parkland were sold to Charles II. The king made few changes to the park and gardens, which continued to deteriorate.

In 1701 William III, who had by then inherited Audley End, was urged in a document from his advisers to rid himself of the property. The document noted that the stable bridge had collapsed into the river, that many of the park walls had fallen, and that the ditches in the park were so 'choket up with mudd: that the curents of water which come through Walden Town are stopt, so that part of the said Towne is over flood'.

Consequently, in November 1701, the house and park were returned to the trustees of the co-heirs of the third Earl of Suffolk.

DECLINE (1708–18)

After a legal dispute the estate was eventually settled on Henry Lord Bindon, who became the owner of Audley End in 1708 and assumed the title sixth Earl of Suffolk in the following year. Despite continued financial insecurity Henry consulted the architect Sir John Vanbrugh, a friend and distant relative, concerning improvements to his newly inherited house. The consultation resulted in a large-scale demolition programme, which included the removal of the Great Kitchen and the north and south wings of the outer court. In keeping with changing fashions, a turning circle for carriages was introduced in the outer court, allowing family and visitors to dismount directly in front of the house. Previously they had had to dismount or disembark at the entrance to the outer court and walk to the main door.

'THE PARK IS PRETTILY IMPROVED AND A VERY GENTEEL SPOT' (1725–33)

In 1725 Charles Howard, the ninth Earl of Suffolk, commissioned a proposal for a vast formal garden, possibly by the French Huguenot architect Nicholas Dubois. However, this plan remained a dream, and a less ambitious scheme was eventually implemented, possibly to a design devised by the king's gardener, Charles Bridgeman. Bridgeman was of the generation before 'Capability' Brown and his gardens incorporated many elements of the formal style. He had been responsible for the design of the famous gardens at Stowe, Buckinghamshire where, appropriately, Brown was soon to follow in his footsteps. The main changes effected by Bridgeman were in the Mount Gardens, where the open grass lawns were planted with high, clipped evergreen hedges intersected with broad pathways. The early seventeenth-century wilderness and cellar gardens were cleared away and a further lawn planted, again flanked and crossed by walkways. Other changes included the demolition of the remaining buildings of the outer court, to be replaced by a low wall topped by railings. At either end of the wall a pair of low pavilions was built, one of which contained a new kitchen linked to the house by an underground tunnel.

The remodelling was probably complete by 1731 when Thomas Robinson wrote in a letter to his father-in-law Lord Carlisle that the park at Audley End 'is prettily improved and a very genteel spot, though of no great extent'.

Despite limited resources the improvements to the park did reflect the fashions of the day: the house became more outward-looking, and its front elevation was no longer obscured by the outer court.

ABOVE *Plan for Audley End, attributed to Charles Bridgeman. Note the turning circle in front of the house*

LEFT *This scene at Stowe shows Charles Bridgeman and Stowe's owner Lord Cobham (seated to left)*

ABOVE *French and Italian landscape paintings such as this, by Claude Lorrain, influenced the development of landscape gardening in England*

ABOVE *Alexander Pope (1688-1744)*

RIGHT *Robert Castell's reconstruction drawing of Pliny's villa in Tuscany (1728)*

FAR RIGHT *Lady Portsmouth. Sir John Griffin Griffin erected an obelisk in the east park in gratitude for her generosity*

'GARDENING IS ... NEARER GOD'S WORK THAN POETRY' (1762–84)

During the late seventeenth and early eighteenth century great formal gardens such as the one at Audley End were coming under increasing criticism. The philosophical ideal of man's mastery of nature was being replaced by the idea of man being at one with his environment. At the same time the expense of creating and maintaining gardens that were purely decorative was questioned. Calls were made to reunite the garden with nature and turn the wasteful acres of the formal garden to more profitable use by introducing grazing and improved forestry techniques. (There were practical reasons for this emphasis on usefulness. Britain's growing population at home and the pursuit of its imperial interests abroad meant that raw materials – especially wood for shipbuilding – were urgently needed.) In terms of social developments, a new sense of equality was reflected in a rejection of the static arrangement of Jacobean gardens in favour of more fluid planning based on circles rather than straight lines.

The campaign was, from the beginning, led by the literary world. The essayist and poet Joseph Addison was a chief exponent, as was the poet and philosopher Alexander Pope, who wrote that 'Gardening is ... nearer God's work than Poetry'. Pope asserted that it was the moral duty of landowners to improve the agriculture and forestry on their estates since these were fundamental to the nation's economy and wellbeing:

> *'Tis use alone that sanctifies expense,*
> *And Splendour borrows all her rays from Sense ...*
> *Whose ample lawns are not asham'd to feed*
> *The milky heifer and deserving steed:*
> *Whose rising Forests, not for pride or show:*
> *But future buildings, future Navies, grow:*
> *Let his plantations stretch from down to down,*
> *First shade a country then raise a town.*

To support their political and aesthetic ideas, Pope and his contemporaries likened the age in which they lived to that of early imperial Rome. (A correlation between the Restoration of Charles II and the reign of the Emperor Augustus following the assassination of Julius Caesar was one of several political comparisons that could be made.) In terms of gardening, examples of classical gardens, where woods and fields formed an integral part of the gardens, were cited to demonstrate the virtues of combining pleasure with productivity. The popularity of ornamenting gardens with 'classical' buildings was a natural development of this theme.

It was not until the mid-eighteenth century, however, that the ideal of an unfettered, natural, and purposeful landscape, adorned with the temples of the ancients, was fulfilled. The translation of a literary idea into reality in some of the greatest gardens in the country was largely the result of the work of the garden designer and architect Lancelot 'Capability' Brown.

ELIZABETH, COUNTESS OF PORTSMOUTH (1745–62)

When the tenth Earl of Suffolk died in 1745 the Howard link with Audley End came to an end. One of the earl's four co-heirs was Elizabeth, Countess of Portsmouth. A woman of strong and generous character, Lady Portsmouth was determined to increase her holding of the estate in order to provide a suitable seat for her nephew and heir, John Griffin Whitwell. In 1751 she purchased the house and immediate park from Lord Effingham, a co-beneficiary. However, she was unable to acquire the land which lay immediately to the west of the house, a failure which would later create a number of problems for her heir.

It was in Lady Portsmouth's time that the first attempts were made to create a less formal landscape. The kitchen gardens were moved to their present location, out of view of the house (a move characteristic of Brown's methods), and the linear driveways which survived from the seventeenth century were given a more flowing form. By this time the avenues planted in the east park during the seventeenth century had mostly been removed (much of the timber having been sold by the impoverished Howards); Lady Portsmouth's gardeners continued to thin out the planting, leaving only individual trees and clumps, through which a herd of some 500 deer roamed.

Lancelot Brown was born of humble origins in the village of Kirkharle in Northumberland in 1715 or early 1716. At the age of sixteen he began working for Sir William Loraine of Kirkharle Hall, who was then carrying out extensive improvements to his estate. Here he probably learnt the basic skills of estate management.

In 1739 Brown moved south, and within two years took up the position of head gardener at Stowe in Buckinghamshire, following in the footsteps of the most celebrated designers of the previous generation, Charles Bridgeman and William Kent. Brown mastered Kent's experiments in informality, grassing over paths and introducing natural outlines to lawns, drives and lakes.

Lancelot Brown. His nickname is said to have arisen from his frequent observation that estates had 'capabilities'

Brown soon started giving advice to the owners of a number of other estates, and, following the death of Stowe's owner Lord Cobham in 1749, he established his own independent practice. From now on he worked tirelessly, travelling vast distances up and down the country to advise landowners on the improvement of their estates.

In 1764 Brown became Master Gardener to George III, carrying out extensive work at Kew Gardens as well as continuing to pursue his independent career. His projects at this time included Thorndon, Wimpole and Burghley, all in the same part of the country as Audley End.

Brown seems to have been on good terms with his clients, who appreciated not only his artistry but also his business-like efficiency and his eye for practicality. He appears to have been a likeable and diplomatic man, succeeding in keeping up good relations with both Whig and Tory clients, as well as with the king. Lord Coventry, whose Worcestershire estate Brown had transformed into a fine park 'out of a morass', remarked after Brown's death in 1783: 'I certainly held him very high as an artist, and esteemed him as a most sincere friend'.

SIR JOHN GRIFFIN GRIFFIN AND 'THE AMUSING CARES OF BUILDING, PLANTING AND DECORATING' (1762–84)

ABOVE *Sir John Griffin Griffin, the moving force behind the landscape park at Audley End*

Lady Portsmouth's Column, completed in 1774

Glass houses were introduced into the extensive kitchen gardens

The Temple of Victory, built in 1774

In 1762 Sir John Griffin Griffin (later fourth Lord Howard de Walden and first Baron Braybrooke) inherited his aunt's estate at Audley End. (His change of name from Whitwell to Griffin was a condition of the inheritance.) Sir John was a career soldier who had served as *aide-de-campe* to George II during the campaigns of the Seven Years' War. He retired to Audley End a man of leisure, eager to channel his considerable energies into new pursuits. Although clearly belonging to a different milieu from the literary and artistic circles which formed the aesthetic tastes of the time, Sir John was interested in the arts and familiar with new ideas: he kept a copy of Pope's *Essay on Man* in the menagerie on the Ring Hill, for example.

On his arrival at Audley End, Sir John immediately set about planning changes to the estate. Like many other wealthy and discerning landowners of the time, he engaged Lancelot Brown to design and carry out improvements to the park and commissioned designs for garden buildings from the Adam brothers. As early as 1762 the diarist Count Frederick Kielmansegge noted that the grounds, though not remarkable, would be improved by the changes the owner was then busy making. Sir John took an exceptional interest in every aspect of the work on his estate; in 1765 William Pitt the Elder (then Prime Minister) remarked in a letter to Sir John that he was no doubt 'deeply engaged in the amusing cares of building, planting and decorating'.

During the next thirty years a transformation was to take place, as the remaining formal features of the seventeenth- and eighteenth-century gardens were buried under tons of rubble and soil, and the stiff formal watercourses and planting of the preceding centuries were removed or remodelled to create a garden in the natural landscape style.

The Elysian Garden, an informal flower garden created in the 1760s, contained various novelties including a cold bath, a tent and a cascade

The Temple of Concord, built in 1790

The river follows a 'serpentine' curve

The public road was concealed by a **Ha Ha,** which also kept livestock inside the park

Exotic birds were kept in the Gothic menagerie (built in 1774)

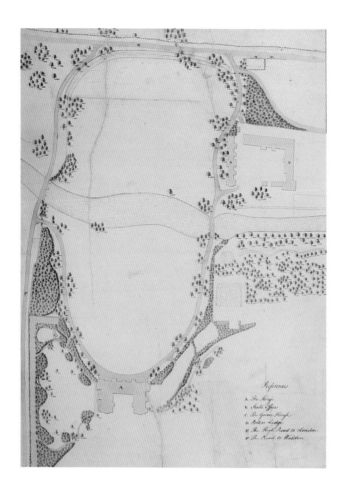

BROWN'S SCHEME FOR AUDLEY END

In 1763 Brown signed a contract with Sir John, in which he undertook to design and carry out the remodelling of the park. Work was concentrated on the west park (the area which incorporated the two public roads) but also entailed extensive changes to the old Mount Garden at the rear of the house.

Although Sir John did not at this point own the upper areas of the west park he intended to acquire them, and the remodelling of these areas seems to have been taken into account. All the garden buildings were conceived at the outset, and Brown presumably had their ultimate positions in mind when he planned them.

One of Brown's skills was to impart an overall conceptual unity to his landscapes, linking individual features into a pleasing whole. Earlier designers had tended to devise a series of separate 'events' which lacked this underlying coherence. The park which was created at Audley End shows many of the characteristic features of Brown's style and is a testament to his artistry – although the path to its completion did not always run smoothly.

THE WEST PARK

It was probably Brown who proposed the planting of belts of trees along the ridges which formed the western and southern horizons of the park. These created the illusion that the west park was a private, secluded space for the exclusive enjoyment of Sir John and his guests. Within this 'enclosed' park Brown created a feeling of spaciousness, with broad, uninterrupted views across the valley and up the slopes to the west and south.

To achieve this effect, the old barriers remaining from the Jacobean gardens were removed and a number of intrusive terraced houses in Audley End High Street were demolished. Instead of fences, Ha Has were introduced: these served the same function but did not interrupt the view, as long as they were positioned at right angles to the line of vision.

The land was gently graded and seeded with grass, producing a smooth sweep of pasture extending from the house right up to the trees on the horizon. Brown used combinations of deciduous and evergreen trees, and always chose species that were native to Britain or at least visually compatible with the British landscape, in keeping with the idea that a landscape park should resemble nature perfected.

THE RIVER AND THE AREA WEST OF THE HOUSE

Brown made the most of Audley End's natural advantages, especially the river which ran through the west park close to the house. He recut the straight Jacobean canal in a leisurely serpentine sweep, and made a virtue of the intrusive road to Walden by introducing a new bridge.

Two sweeping carriage drives were introduced and new entrance gateways with porter's lodges were proposed at the end of each drive. In the event, the new gates and lodges were not built in the course of Brown's work at Audley End.

LADY GRIFFIN'S GARDEN

Ever practical, Brown often included a 'close walk' or 'pleasure ground' (an area of concentrated interest) within easy reach of the house to provide a place for walking and entertainment in poor weather. At Audley End the pleasure ground, or Lady Griffin's Garden as it was known, was situated on the north, east and south sides of the house. It was informal in style and was protected from the elements, and from the eyes of the public, by a screen of evergreens. A Ha Ha was introduced along the north and east sides of the garden to keep out the sheep and cattle that grazed the park beyond.

During the creation of Lady Griffin's Garden the area to the south of the house was transformed, though elements of the Jacobean Mount Garden were retained. Two curving paths lined with evergreens were introduced, leading from the south side of the house to the elevated Jacobean walkway.

At the northern end of the pleasure grounds an ornamental dairy was built. A popular feature of eighteenth-century gardens, ornamental dairies were visited by guests during their tour of the park. The mistress of the house often supervised their running.

The pleasure grounds provided a discreet, shady retreat which could be reached directly from the apartments newly remodelled by Robert Adam in the south wing of the house.

THE CONTRACT

The contract which Sir John had agreed with Brown in 1763 outlined seven specific items of work. Sir John agreed to provide trees, shrubs, carts, wheelbarrows, four able horses and harnesses, and labour costs while Brown was to provide the design and supervise the work. Brown undertook to complete his contract between 22 April 1763 and May 1764 and was to receive a total of £660 paid in three instalments, the final instalment being paid on completion. When May arrived, however, the work was still unfinished.

Despite this, Sir John released Brown from his contractual obligations and continued to make payments of £200 per annum until 1766, when Brown submitted his final bill. This bill, however, included £94 9s 4d in interest, to which Sir John took exception.

There followed a long and bitter dispute which resulted in an irrevocable rift between the two, and ultimately saw an end to Brown's supervision of the landscape works at Audley End.

LEFT The Brockman family and friends at Beachborough Manor, by Edward Hartley, 1743–60. This painting shows a landscape park as the setting for various leisurely pursuits

LEFT Lady Griffin's Garden was created for Sir John's first wife, Anna Maria Schutz

THE VISTAS

During the early 1770s work began on the construction of a number of ornamental buildings, largely conceived in the previous decade. These were positioned at the outer perimeters of the park to the west, south and east, and formed focal points which could be seen from afar. A party making a tour or 'circuit' of the estate had the added excitement of being able to see these buildings at close quarters: they might stop off to take tea, listen to music and play cards, or simply to enjoy deciphering the inscriptions and motifs adorning both exteriors and interiors.

RIGHT Adam's design drawing for the Temple of Victory (1771). The twelve Ionic capitals (at the tops of the columns) were carved in Portland Stone at a cost of £49 12s

BELOW A harp was kept at the temple for the entertainment of guests

VISTAS IN THE WEST PARK

The Temple of Victory dominates the view in the west park. It was designed by Robert Adam and is modelled on Palladio's reconstruction drawing of the Temple of Vesta at the Villa d'Este, Tivoli. It was begun in 1774 and commemorates the British victory over France and Spain during the Seven Years' War (1756–63).

Inside is an elaborately decorated domed plaster ceiling modelled by Joseph Rose and Co, probably the most eminent firm of decorative plaster craftsmen of the period.

The ceiling was created using a contraption known as 'The Machine' which consisted of a central pivot with radiating arms. The arms held boards cut to the profile of the dome, which the craftsmen pushed round at speed, skimming the plaster to the correct shape as they went.

The ceiling decoration comprises six medallions (roundels) carrying images of Roman gods and goddesses. These illustrate the theme of war and its consequences. The last figure, Fame, records the events of the war on a large oval tablet. At the same point on the outside of the temple, as though

1 STRENGTH
  (Minerva and Mars)
2 JUSTICE
3 VICTORY
  (shown with Hercules)
4 PEACE
5 SECURITAS
6 FAME

LEFT *Roundels on the ceiling of the Temple of Victory. Taken together, they embody the message that with strength and justice come victory, peace, security and, finally, fame*

actually written by Fame, a stone tablet bears the following inscription:

SACRED TO VICTORY

Eminently Triumphant

In Europe, Asia, Africa And America

By The Glorious And Unparalleled Successes

Of The British Fleets And Armies

In The War Commenced M.DCC.LV [1755]

Concluded M.DCC.LXII [1763]

When France And Spain

Making Overtures

To The Crown Of Great Britain

And Yielding

To The Superiority Of Her Arms

PEACE WAS RESTORED.

The temple was furnished with five curved settees and a table with a marble base decorated with rams' heads, all designed by Robert Adam.

Not far from the Temple of Victory was another attraction, the menagerie (not open to the public). Here visitors were entertained by the sight of a multitude of unusual and exotic birds. Multi-coloured pheasants strutted across the open lawns enclosed by high walls, while the building itself housed eagles, parrots, canaries and goldfinches, amongst others.

The menagerie was completed in 1774 and is designed in the Gothic style. Inside it was divided into three rooms: the kitchen, Tea Room and Bird Room. An inventory of 1797 noted that the Tea Room contained '4 Painted Chairs, 4 Wood Stools, a Matt. Circular table, Prints affixed on sides, 1 Shagreen Writing case, 12 Silver Tea Spoons. 1 pair Tongs, 1 do Tea Pot. Cups and Saucers, a Hand Bell and Tea Chest' and the following books: *Catesby, Carolina,* Pope's *Essay on Man, The Complete Grazier* and a *Natural History of Songs of Birds.* Visitors could see directly into the Bird Room from the Tea Room.

Menageries were a popular feature of eighteenth-century parks, often containing exotic animals as well as birds. The birds not only provided entertainment but were a source of scientific interest. A number of the birds from the menagerie now form part of the natural history collection inside Audley End House.

MARY EVANS PICTURE LIBRARY

VISTAS IN THE EAST PARK

In 1774 a memorial dedicated to the memory of Lady Portsmouth was erected in the east park. Finally, in 1790, work began on the last of the major monuments to be built during Sir John's lifetime, the Temple of Concord (see p.17).

ABOVE *The Temple of Concord, painted in the late eighteenth century. A wrought-iron bridge allowed visitors to cross the encircling Ha Ha*

THE KITCHEN GARDEN

Following Brown's departure Sir John appointed a new superviser, Joseph Hicks, to oversee work in the east park. Under Hicks, roads were removed, grass seeded and the slope of the park graded.

Before this work began, however, Sir John turned his attention towards the creation of a modern kitchen garden. In 1768 new brick enclosure walls were built against the existing kitchen garden (dating from Lady Portsmouth's time) and numerous glass houses were built along the southern wall. These were heated by a series of horizontal flues inside the brick walls which were fired by coal furnaces. The hot walls, glazing, and a further heating device involving a series of pits heated by the warmth of decaying vegetation, provided suitable growing conditions for flowers, fruit and vegetables.

In the early 1770s a greenhouse (now demolished) was built in Lady Portsmouth's kitchen garden. It was designed in the classical style by John Hobcroft, the carpenter also responsible for the design and construction of the Gothic chapel inside the house. The greenhouse was probably used for overwintering orange trees which would be brought out into the gardens in their tubs in summer. It was flanked by glass houses in which vines were grown.

THE ELYSIAN GARDEN

In the early 1780s Sir John embarked on the creation of a further pleasure ground, in the form of a new informal flower garden to the north-west of the house, near the site of the water mill. The Elysian fields, after which the garden was named, were in classical mythology the abode of the blessed after death – a place of ideal or perfect happiness.

The proposals for the new garden included various features: a Doric arcade, a cold bath, a subterranean passage, a rustic gateway and a cascade. The initial plan was produced by the garden designer and architect Richard Woods, but an alternative scheme was later commissioned from Placido Columbani, a designer in Robert Adam's circle. Columbani proposed – and probably built – a cold bath fronted by 'Rock Work, or old roots of trees and Moss', as opposed to Woods's cold bath, housed in a temple-like pavilion.

The completed garden had many pleasures to offer. Even the entrance provided an unusual and thrilling experience. A rustic gateway led into a subterranean arch, then to a second gate, possibly Gothic in style. Visitors would progress along this gloomy route lined with evergreens until eventually

RIGHT *Scheme for the Elysian Garden, attributed to Columbani*

LEFT *The Elysian Garden, by William Tomkins, 1788. The garden was a bright open glade sheltered by dark evergreens*

they emerged dramatically into the open glade of the Elysian Garden. (There was a more pragmatic explanation for the tunnel. A trackway ran across the top of the subterranean arch allowing cattle, hay and dung carts to pass through the garden on their way from the stable area to the fields without soiling the footpaths.)

One of the first sights that greeted visitors as they emerged into the garden was a blue-and-white canvas tent, which provided shade and a pleasant retreat in which to take refreshments. A series of circuitous paths was laid out around the garden with sweet-smelling and exotic flowers planted alongside. Stone statues appeared at various intervals, and flowering trees and shrubs were planted liberally, including roses, magnolias and rhododendrons.

Columbani noted that the garden would 'cherish every plant', since it provided a sheltered situation, had rich soil and an ample supply of water. Sadly, in the event it proved to be a frost trap and failed to flourish as had been envisaged.

By the 1830s the planting, gateways, subterranean arch and tent had all been demolished or removed and the arrangement of the garden simplified.

THE END OF AN ERA

In 1786 there was a possibility that George III might visit Audley End on his way to Cambridge. In the event the visit never materialised, but this did not prevent frenzied preparations taking place over the summer. The Lion Gate, which had already been remodelled in about 1768, was further refurbished (see p.5).

By 1783 the planting, building and remodelling of the park had largely been completed. A survey made that year shows the park much as Brown must have intended it: the boundaries on the higher ground are lined with belts of trees, while buildings of contrasting styles are carefully dispersed about the grounds. Miss Emilia Clayton, Lady Howard's half-sister, was sufficiently impressed to write to a correspondent in October 1786: 'The fine grounds, which really are delightful, are vastly improved since last we were here'. Under Sir John's stewardship the old formal grounds had finally disappeared and in their place was a varied, entertaining and productive landscape in the best tradition of the 'natural' style.

ABOVE *A flower garden was an unusual feature at the time, probably inspired by Lord Harcourt's famous 'Elysian Garden' at Nuneham Courtney, Oxfordshire*

LEFT *Azaleas and geraniums were amongst the flowers prescribed by Columbani for the Elysian Garden*

THE NINETEENTH CENTURY AND THE RETURN OF FORMALITY

Sir John Griffin Griffin died without immediate heirs in 1794. The next owner to make important changes in the park was Richard Neville, the third Lord Braybrooke, who inherited Audley End in 1825 and came to live there with his wife Jane and their eight children.

Since Sir John's time gardening fashions had changed, and the classical buildings in the park must have seemed quite alien to early nineteenth-century taste. The classical world and its pagan deities had lost their appeal in favour of traditional 'Englishness' and an idealised national past, underpinned by Christian convictions. (The French Revolution had shaken the English aristocracy to its foundations and freedom and 'naturalness' seemed to have gone too far: the reaction was a renewed desire for order, but also a new emphasis on the comfort and happiness of employees – a noticeable feature of nineteenth-century developments at Audley End.)

On inheriting the estate, Lord Braybrooke began a series of alterations to the house and park. He had already made a study of the history of the family and now aimed to reinstate the Jacobean character of his ancestral seat. He and Lady Braybrooke had visited parks and palaces throughout England and the Continent in search of inspiration. (In the event, their ambitions were scaled down, and many of the eighteenth-century features of the house and park remained intact.)

THE PARTERRE

As part of his scheme of alteration, Lord Braybrooke created a formal flower garden or parterre at the rear of the house. This was intended to complement changes that were taking place inside the house, where a library in the Jacobean style was being created on the first floor of the south wing. From here the elaborate patterns of the flower beds could be seen to best effect.

In fact, the Suffolk parterres at Audley End only ever consisted of simple grass beds, but the fashionable revival of Jacobean features favoured a more flamboyant approach. Advice on the garden was given by the eminent nineteenth-century garden designer William Sawrey Gilpin, though the design itself was taken from an eighteenth-century garden pattern book.

Preparations for the construction of the new garden were probably under way by 1831, in which year the estate's expenditure on plants and seeds doubled. The flower beds were cut in geometric shapes, and great care was taken to cause minimal disturbance to the buried remains of the abbey which lay below.

ABOVE *Richard Neville, third Lord Braybrooke (1783–1858)*

RIGHT *The original layout of the parterre was confirmed by archaeological excavation, which also helped to establish the size of the former abbey*

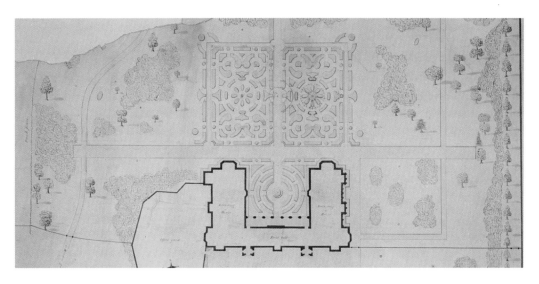

During the mid-1980s English Heritage investigated the feasibility of restoring the garden to its mid-nineteenth-century appearance. Extensive research and a pioneering project in garden archaeology were undertaken. The studies revealed the form of the garden and the plants it had contained, and the decision was taken to go ahead with the restoration. Work began in October 1989 with the laying out of the beds to the original plan, and the planting took place the following spring. As a result of this project Lord Braybrooke's colourful reinterpretation of Jacobean formality can be enjoyed once again.

THE KITCHEN GARDENS

During the nineteenth century substantial changes were made in the kitchen gardens. Sir John's greenhouses were demolished and an extensive vine house was built in 1802 on the site of Sir John's orangery. A number of other greenhouses were added, including an orchard house (now demolished), designed specifically for fruit-growing. The fruit trees were placed on large wheeled benches which sat on rails and could be drawn out into the open at certain times of year to take advantage of the fresh air.

Records show that in 1884 apricots, peaches, nectarines and plums were being grown against the garden walls.

There were about 2,600 strawberry plants and several types of pineapple. Over 250 varieties of chrysanthemum were produced, as well as primula simensis, alba plena and salvias, such as Gesneri Flora, Pseudo Cocinea, Crotons and Dracanas.

Lord Braybrooke kept his thoroughbreds in the paddocks of the kitchen gardens. The most famous of these, Sir Joshua, won the 1000 Guineas in April 1816 by beating the winner of the St Leger, Filho de Puta. At about this date the stables were fitted out with loose boxes.

THE PARK

In 1811 a herd of Alderney cows was introduced into the park – the foundation of what was to become recognised as the oldest Jersey herd in England. Besides providing milk, the cattle were regularly entered for competitions and studied for scientific interest.

During the 1840s and '50s two new lodges were built at the main entrances to the park (see pages 6 and 10).

MANSELL COLLECTION

THE POND GARDEN

A new garden – the Pond Garden – was created for the fifth Lord Braybrooke in about 1865 between the kitchen garden and the old Elysian Garden (see p.11). It was inspired by the mid-nineteenth-century romantic taste for rugged landscapes and raging torrents of water. A torrent could be made to rush through a channel alongside the garden by opening a series of sluice gates. A rockery, intended to be reminiscent of popular wild landscapes such as those of the Lake District, was constructed at the southern end of the garden.

LEFT *The parterre fell out of use during the Second World War and deteriorated into a very poor state*

LEFT *'Dr Syntax' sketching Lake Windermere. A mid-nineteenth-century parody of the taste for the picturesque*

LEFT *These fruits are varieties known to have been grown at Audley End in the nineteenth century*

THE PARK IN THE TWENTIETH CENTURY

Few changes were made in the park and gardens during the early twentieth century. At the outbreak of the Second World War the house and park were requisitioned by the army. Large areas of the park were ploughed up and planted with crops to provide desperately needed food supplies.

During much of this period the house was used by the Polish section of the Special Operations Executive, whose agents were air-dropped into German-occupied Poland. A memorial urn was later placed in the west park, near the Lion Gate, to honour the men from this unit who were killed on active service.

Audley End was derequisitioned in 1945 and in 1948 the house passed to the State in

lieu of death duties. It was first opened to the public in 1950, and is now looked after by English Heritage.

Maintaining the gardens and park is an ongoing process: the trees and planting schemes require constant attention and the buildings need frequent repairs. In addition to maintenance, more ambitious projects have recently been carried out. Most spectacularly, the nineteenth-century parterre has been restored in a pioneering project combining archaeological investigation and documentary research.

Today Audley End park retains much of the form and appearance of the magnificent eighteenth-century landscape created by 'Capability' Brown. Of all the schemes that have been devised for Audley End this was the boldest, the most ambitious and innovative. Yet within this overall, unified scheme, there are striking reminders of other periods in Audley End's history. These are sometimes little more than fleeting glimpses of vanished gardens; or remnants of the more limited schemes introduced by owners living in less confident times. Nevertheless they are a potent reminder of the alternative philosophical and aesthetic beliefs that inspired their creators.

Although some areas of the park have lost their former splendour, the gardens have benefited greatly from the sustained attention they have received in recent decades. Despite the changes wrought by time, the spirit and form of the eighteenth-century park survive.

RIGHT *Audley End opens to the public, 1950*

BELOW *The Polish memorial urn in the west park*